PIANO • VOCAL • GUITAR

2ND EDITION

WEDDING SONGS
Country Style

ISBN 0-7935-7243-6

HAL•LEONARD®
CORPORATION

7777 W. BLUEMOUND RD. P.O. BOX 13819 MILWAUKEE, WI 53213

Visit Hal Leonard Online at
www.halleonard.com

AMAZED

Words and Music by CHRIS LINDSEY,
MARV GREEN and AIMEE MAYO

Moderately slow Country Ballad

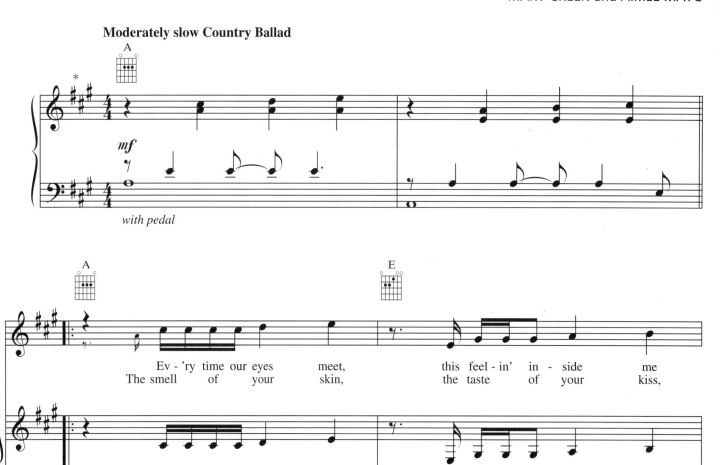

with pedal

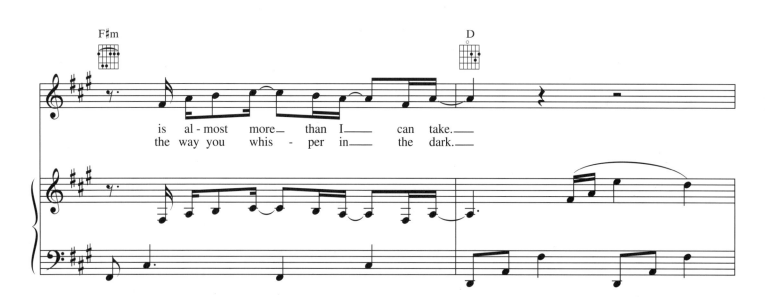

Ev - 'ry time our eyes meet, this feel - in' in - side me
The smell of your skin, the taste of your kiss,

is al - most more— than I— can take.—
the way you whis - per in— the dark.—

*Recorded a half step lower.

THE BATTLE HYMN OF LOVE

Words and Music by DON SCHLITZ
and PAUL OVERSTREET

AMEN KIND OF LOVE

Words and Music by TREY BRUCE
and WAYNE TESTER

We are moved _____ by the spir - it.

CAN'T HELP FALLING IN LOVE

from the Paramount Picture BLUE HAWAII

Words and Music by GEORGE DAVID WEISS,
HUGO PERETTI and LUIGI CREATORE

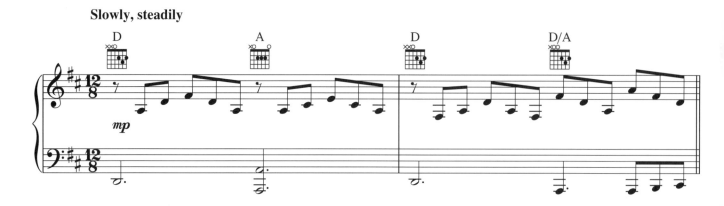

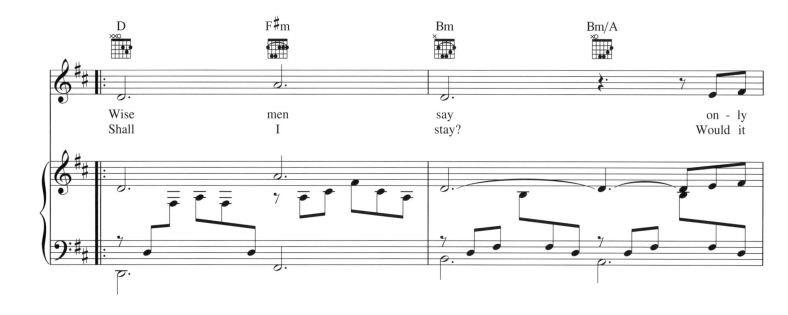

Wise men say only
Shall I stay?

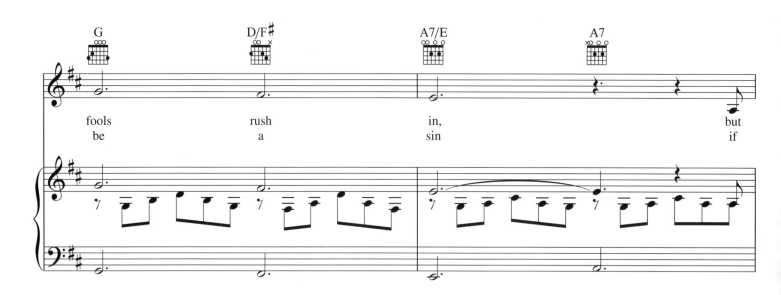

fools rush in, but
be a sin if

COULD I HAVE THIS DANCE

from URBAN COWBOY

Words and Music by WAYLAND HOLYFIELD
and BOB HOUSE

I'll al-ways re-mem-ber the song they were
al-ways re-mem-ber that mag-ic

play-ing, the first time _____ we danced and I knew.
mo-ment, when I held _____ you close to me.

As we swayed to the mu-sic _____ and held to each
As we moved to-geth-er, _____ I knew for-

FOREVER AND EVER, AMEN

Words and Music by PAUL OVERSTREET
and DON SCHLITZ

Lively Country

mf

You may think that I'm ___
time takes its I'm toll ___

___ talk-in' fool-ish,
___ on a bod-y,

you've
makes a

heard that I'm wild ___ and I'm free. ___
young gi-rl's brown ___ hair ___ turn gray.

Oh ba - by, }
Oh dar - lin', } I'm gon - na love _____ you for - ev -

- er, _____ for - ev - er and ev -

- er, a - men. _____ As

long as old men _____ sit and talk a - bout _____ the weath -

-er, as long as old wom - en sit and

talk a - bout ___ old ___ men; if you won - der how long ___

___ I'll be faith - ful,

I'll be
well, just

hap - py to tell ___ you a - gain. ___
lis - ten to how ___ this song ends;

FROM HERE TO ETERNITY

Words and Music by ROBERT ELLIS ORRALL
and MICHAEL PETERSON

FROM THIS MOMENT ON

Words and Music by SHANIA TWAIN
and R.J. LANGE

* Male vocals sung an octave higher throughout.

GROW OLD WITH ME

Words and Music by
JOHN LENNON

Moderate Ballad

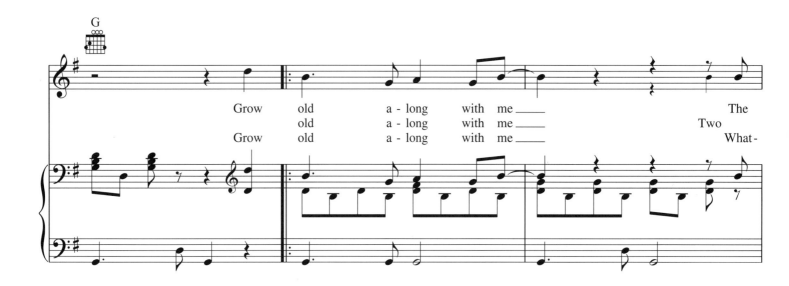

Grow old a-long with me _____
old a-long with me _____ The Two
Grow old a-long with me _____ What-

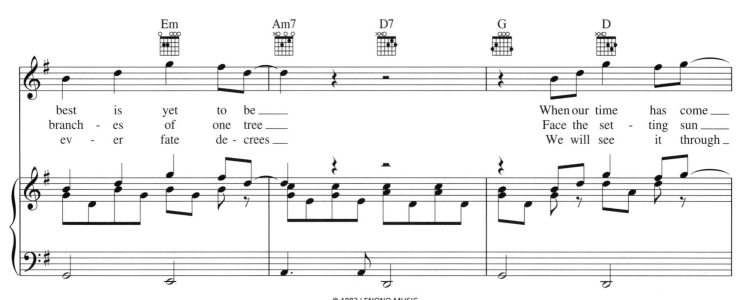

best is yet to be _____ When our time has come _____
branch - es of one tree _____ Face the set - ting sun _____
ev - er fate de - crees _____ We will see it through _

I CAN LOVE YOU LIKE THAT

Words and Music by MARIBETH DERRY,
JENNIFER KIMBALL and STEVE DIAMOND

You want ten - der - ness, I got ten -

- der - ness. And I see through __ to the

heart of you. __ If you want a man who un - der - stands, __

you don't have to look ver - y far. _____

I JUST FALL IN LOVE AGAIN

Words and Music by LARRY HERBSTRITT,
STEPHEN H. DORFF, GLORIA SKLEROV
and HARRY LLOYD

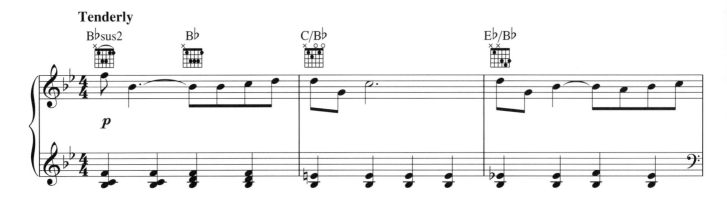

Dream-in', I must _ be dream-in', or
Mag-ic, it must _ be mag-ic, the way I

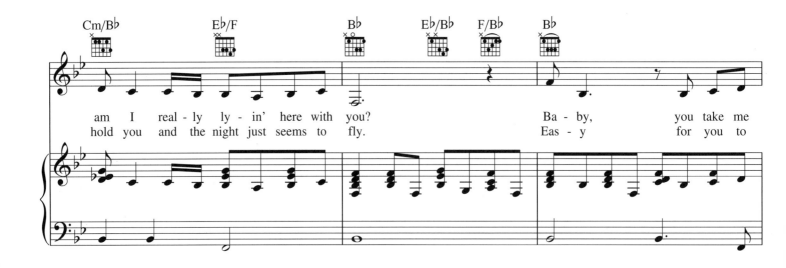

am I real-ly ly-in' here with you?   Ba-by, you take me
hold you and the night just seems to fly.   Eas-y for you to

I NEED YOU

Words and Music by DENNIS MATKOSKY
and TY LACY

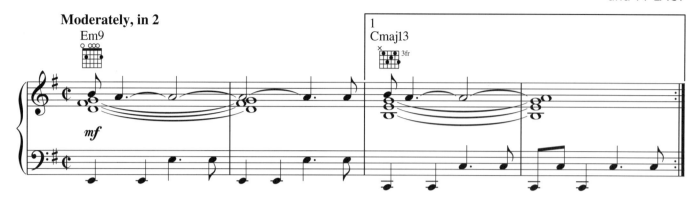

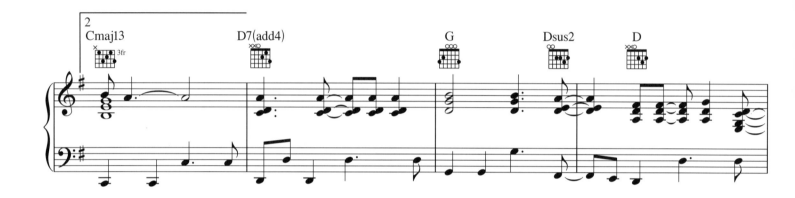

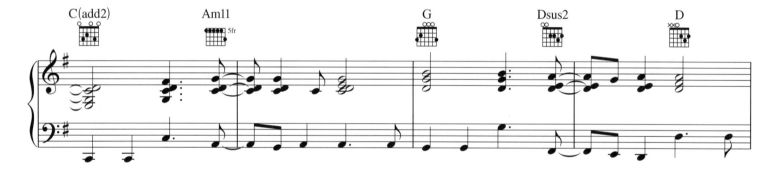

I don't need a lot ___ of things; I can

*Vocal line written one octave higher than sung.

60

I NEVER KNEW LOVE

Words and Music by WILL ROBINSON
and LARRY BOONE

I nev-er knew the pow-er ____ of a song ____
I nev-er un-der-stood the mean-ing of home ____

till I heard the mu-sic play-in' the day
till I pulled in-to ____ that old dirt drive af-ter

I SWEAR

Words and Music by FRANK MYERS
and GARY BAKER

I see the ques - tions in____ your eyes;____ I know what's weigh -
I'll give you ev - 'ry - thing____ I can;____ I'll build your dreams

I.O.U.

Words and Music by KERRY CHATER
and AUSTIN ROBERTS

Moderately slow Ballad

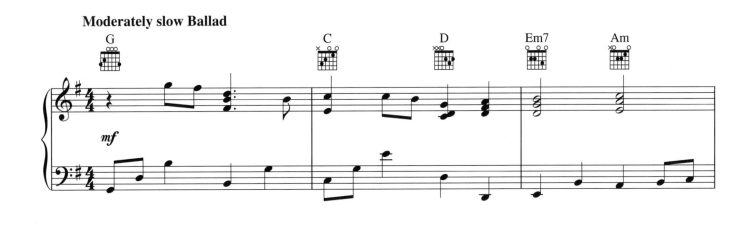

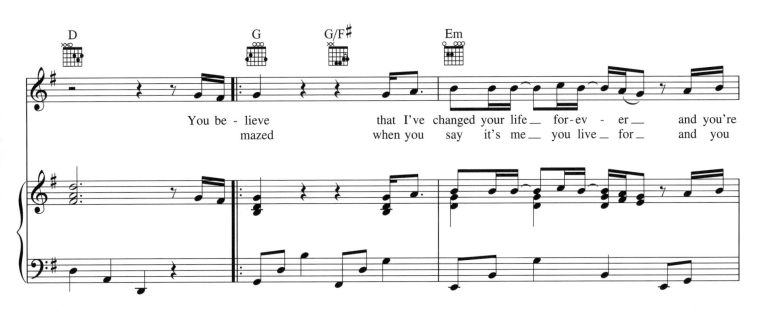

You be - lieve ____ that I've changed your life ____ for-ev - er ____ and you're
mazed ____ when you say it's me ____ you live ____ for ____ and you

nev - er gon - na find ____ an - oth - er some-bod - y like me. ____ And you
know that when ____ I'm hold - ing you, you're right where you be - long. ____ And, my

I'LL STILL BE LOVING YOU

Words and Music by TODD CERNEY, PAM ROSE,
MARYANN KENNEDY and PAT BUNCH

IT'S YOUR LOVE

Words and Music by
STEPHONY E. SMITH

THE KEEPER OF THE STARS

Words and Music by KAREN STALEY,
DANNY MAYO and DICKEY LEE

LOVE REMAINS

Words and Music by TOM DOUGLAS
and JIM DADDARIO

LOVE CAN BUILD A BRIDGE

Words and Music by PAUL OVERSTREET,
JOHN JARVIS and NAOMI JUDD

LOVE ME TENDER

Words and Music by ELVIS PRESLEY
and VERA MATSON

LOVE WITHOUT END, AMEN

Words and Music by
AARON G. BARKER

MARRY ME

Words and Music by NEIL DIAMOND
and TOM SHAPIRO

NO DOUBT ABOUT IT

Words and Music by JOHN SCOTT SHERRILL
and STEVE SESKIN

NOBODY LOVES ME LIKE YOU DO

Words by PAMELA PHILLIPS
Music by JAMES P. DUNNE

Female: Like a can - dle burn - ing bright,

love is glow - ing in ___ your eyes. ___

NO PLACE THAT FAR

Words and Music by SARA EVANS,
TOM SHAPIRO and TONY MARTIN

There's ___ no place ___ that far. ___

Ba - by, there's no place ___ that ___

far. ___

NOW AND FOREVER
(You and Me)

Words and Music by JIM VALLANCE,
RANDY GOODRUM and DAVID FOSTER

Moderately slow Rock

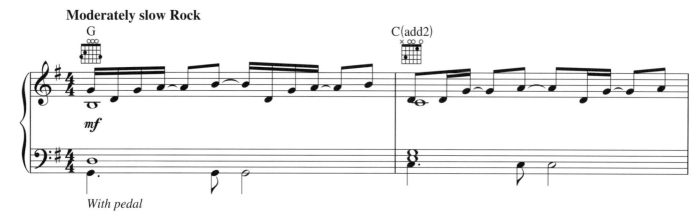

With pedal

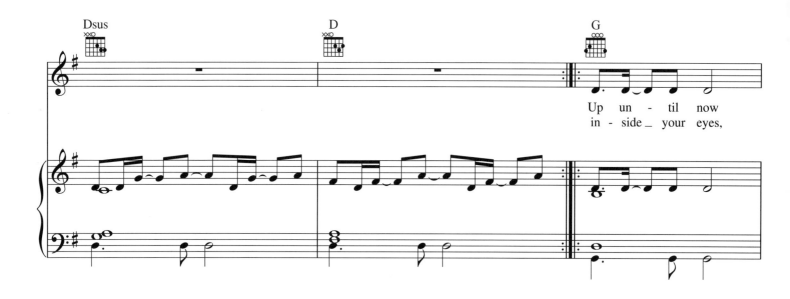

Up un - til now
in - side _ your eyes,

I've learned to live _ with - out love,
I can see mys - ter - ies there.

one thing that I'm _____ so sure _____ of.

Instrumental solo

Solo ends I feel you in - side _____ my soul, _____ and I'm cap - tured _____ to - night. But don't let _____ go. _____ This is par - a - dise.

ONE BOY, ONE GIRL

Words and Music by MARK ALAN SPRINGER
and SHAYE SMITH

SHE IS HIS ONLY NEED

Words and Music by
DAVE LOGGINS

With a relaxed feel

Bil - ly was a small town lon - er ___ who nev - er did dream ___

of ev - er leav - ing south - ern Ar - i - zo - na ___ or ev - er hear - ing wed - ding bells ___ ring.

Bil - ly watch -ing Bon - nie's hair ___ turn gray. And ev -'ry once in a while you could

see him get up ___ and he'd ___ head ___ down - town 'cause he'd heard a - bout some - thing she'd want - ed ___

___ and it just had ___ to be found. ___ Did - n't mat - ter how sim - ple or how much. It was

love. ___ And boy, ain't that love just some - thing

PLEDGING MY LOVE

Words and Music by DON ROBEY
and FATS WASHINGTON

THROUGH THE YEARS

Words and Music by STEVE DORFF
and MARTY PANZER

THE VOWS GO UNBROKEN
(Always True to You)

Words and Music by GARY BURR
and ERIC KAZ

WHEN YOU SAY NOTHING AT ALL

Words and Music by DON SCHLITZ
and PAUL OVERSTREET

Moderately slow

It's a-maz-ing how you can speak right to my heart.
All day long I can hear peo-ple talk-ing out loud,

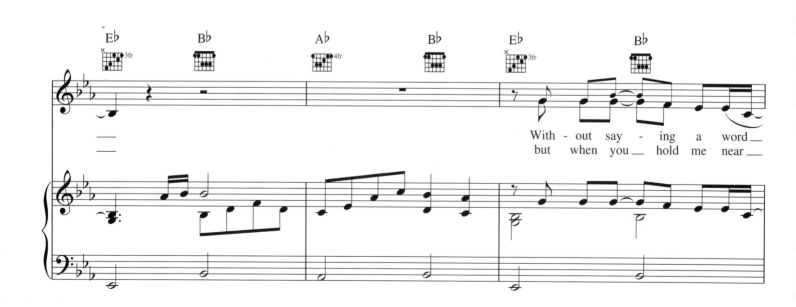

With-out say-ing a word
but when you hold me near

YEARS FROM NOW

Words and Music by ROGER COOK
and CHARLES COCHRAN

YOU NEEDED ME

Words and Music by
RANDY GOODRUM

The Most Romantic Music In The World

Arranged for piano, voice, and guitar

The Best Love Songs Ever - 2nd Edition

This revised edition includes 65 romantic favorites: Always • Beautiful in My Eyes • Can You Feel the Love Tonight • Endless Love • Have I Told You Lately • Misty • Something • Through the Years • Truly • When I Fall in Love • and more.

00359198 ....$19.95

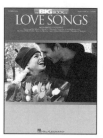

The Big Book of Love Songs - 2nd Edition

80 romantic hits in many musical styles: Always on My Mind • Cherish • Fields of Gold • I Honestly Love You • I'll Be There • Isn't It Romantic? • Lady • My Heart Will Go On • Save the Best for Last • Truly • Wonderful Tonight • and more.

00310784 ....$19.95

The Christian Wedding Songbook

37 songs of love and commitment, including: Bonded Together • Cherish the Treasure • Flesh of My Flesh • Go There with You • Household of Faith • How Beautiful • I Will Be Here • Love Will Be Our Home • Make Us One • Parent's Prayer • This Is the Day • This Very Day • and more.

00310681 ....$16.95

The Bride's Guide to Wedding Music

This great guide is a complete resource for planning wedding music. It includes a thorough article on choosing music for a wedding ceremony, and 65 songs in many different styles to satisfy lots of different tastes. The songs are grouped by categories, including preludes, processionals, recessionals, traditional sacred songs, popular songs, country songs, contemporary Christian songs, Broadway numbers, and new age piano music.

00310615 ....$19.95

Broadway Love Songs

50 romantic favorites from shows such as *Phantom of the Opera*, *Guys and Dolls*, *Oklahoma!*, *South Pacific*, *Fiddler on the Roof* and more. Songs include: All I Ask of You • Bewitched • I've Grown Accustomed to Her Face • Love Changes Everything • So in Love • Sunrise, Sunset • Unexpected Song • We Kiss in a Shadow • and more.

00311558 ....$15.95

Country Love Songs - 4th Edition

This edition features 34 romantic country favorites: Amazed • Breathe • Could I Have This Dance • Forever and Ever, Amen • I Need You • The Keeper of the Stars • Love Can Build a Bridge • One Boy, One Girl • Stand by Me • This Kiss • Through the Years • Valentine • You Needed Me • more.

00311528 ....$14.95

The Definitive Love Collection - 2nd Edition

100 romantic favorites — all in one convenient collection! Includes: All I Ask of You • Can't Help Falling in Love • Endless Love • The Glory of Love • Have I Told You Lately • Heart and Soul • Lady in Red • Love Me Tender • My Romance • So in Love • Somewhere Out There • Unforgettable • Up Where We Belong • When I Fall in Love • and more!

00311681 ....$24.95

I Will Be Here

Over two dozen romantic selections from top contemporary Christian artists such as Susan Ashton, Avalon, Steven Curtis Chapman, Twila Paris, Sonicflood, and others. Songs include: Answered Prayer • Beautiful in My Eyes • Celebrate You • For Always • Give Me Forever (I Do) • Go There with You • How Beautiful • Love Will Be Our Home • and more.

00306472 ....$17.95

Love Songs
Budget Books Series

74 favorite love songs, including: And I Love Her • Cherish • Crazy • Endless Love • Fields of Gold • I Just Called to Say I Love You • I'll Be There • (You Make Me Feel Like) A Natural Woman • Wonderful Tonight • You Are So Beautiful • and more.

00310834 ....$12.95

The New Complete Wedding Songbook

41 of the most requested and beloved songs for romance and weddings: Anniversary Song • Ave Maria • Canon in D (Pachelbel) • Could I Have This Dance • Endless Love • I Love You Truly • Just the Way You Are • The Lord's Prayer • Through the Years • You Needed Me • Your Song • and more.

00309326 ....$12.95

New Ultimate Love and Wedding Songbook

This whopping songbook features 90 songs of devotion, including: The Anniversary Waltz • Can't Smile Without You • Could I Have This Dance • Endless Love • For All We Know • Forever and Ever, Amen • The Hawaiian Wedding Song • Here, There and Everywhere • I Only Have Eyes for You • Just the Way You Are • Longer • The Lord's Prayer • Love Me Tender • Misty • Somewhere • Sunrise, Sunset • Through the Years • Trumpet Voluntary • Your Song • and more.

00361445 ....$19.95

Romance - Boleros Favoritos

Features 48 Spanish and Latin American favorites: Aquellos Ojos Verdes • Bésame Mucho • El Reloj • Frenes • Inolvidable • La Vida Es Un Sueño • Perfidia • Siempre En Mi Corazón • Solamente Una Vez • more.

00310383 ....$16.95

Soulful Love Songs

Features 35 favorite romantic ballads, including: All My Life • Baby, Come to Me • Being with You • Endless Love • Hero • I Just Called to Say I Love You • I'll Make Love to You • I'm Still in Love with You • Killing Me Softly with His Song • My Cherie Amour • My Eyes Adored You • Oh Girl • On the Wings of Love • Overjoyed • Tonight, I Celebrate My Love • Vision of Love • You Are the Sunshine of My Life • You've Made Me So Very Happy • and more.

00310922 ....$14.95

Selections from
VH1's 100 Greatest Love Songs

Nearly 100 love songs chosen for their emotion. Includes: Always on My Mind • Baby, I Love Your Way • Careless Whisper • Endless Love • How Deep Is Your Love • I Got You Babe • If You Leave Me Now • Love Me Tender • My Heart Will Go On • Unchained Melody • You're Still the One • and dozens more!

00306506 ....$27.95